GREED IS GOOD - SO IS SOCIALISM:
A UNIFYING MANIFESTO

Wendell H. Williams

To Roger,
one of my Earliest
Supporter.
Wendell

outskirtspress
DENVER, COLORADO

GREED IS GOOD - SO IS SOCIALISM
A Unifying Manifesto
All Rights Reserved.
Copyright © 2014 Wendell H. Williams
v4.0

Outskirts Press, Inc.
http://www.outskirtspress.com

ISBN: 978-1-4787-3359-1

Outskirts Press and the "OP" logo are trademarks belonging to Outskirts Press, Inc.

PRINTED IN THE UNITED STATES OF AMERICA

TABLE OF CONTENTS

To Judith, my wife and political compatriot

FOREWORD

"If you laid all the economists end to end
to tell you which way to go, they would look like
the spokes of a wheel"

Harry Truman

FEAR OF SOCIALISM

Most Americans appear to be more afraid of the word socialism than the plague. So let me quickly explain what I mean by socialism. I am not talking about the old fashioned socialism tried in the Soviet Union where the government owned the land and factories and planned the economy. No, I am talking about a system of social welfare for the common good that also includes corporate, farm and welfare subsidies, as well as regulations.

Specifically, what I mean and advocate is any governmental expenditure where the return on investment (ROI) to society as a whole is greater than the cost to society as a whole. For lack of a better name, let's just call it "Democratic Social Capitalism." And by the word "greed" I mean self-interest over any concern for society or the commonwealth as a whole. When people are asked to define capitalism and socialism, they have trouble defining either one, which makes comparing them with each other difficult. However in 2012-14, there is a great interest among Americans about this subject. Wikipedia reported last year that the two most often looked up words in the English language were socialism and capitalism. And why? The American people sense that something is not working right any more in our capitalistic economic system. They are just not sure what it is. Furthermore, we need to stop thinking of capitalism and socialism as two discrete options, black or white, as if we are forced to choose one over the other instead of considering a blend of the two; shades of gray if you will. There are gradients between pure capitalism and pure socialism. There is a continuum between these polar opposites, affording a great many variations by mixing them. We don't need to replace capitalism with socialism. But we do need to "tweak" capitalism with enough socialistic laws to prevent runaway income disparity between the rich and poor. Socialism need not be contradictory to capitalism; it can be complimentary.

How did we gradually get to the point where we, a supposedly moral and democratic society, believe that it is morally acceptable for one family, like the Waltons, to have acquired their wealth by paying their employees a near minimum wage that is not even a living wage, while they amass a fortune that is equal to the combined wealth of that of the lower 25% of all Americans. And even though Walmart employees spend the majority of their day at work, they have no say in the management of the company. Is that "democratic"? Walmart recently shocked the world by suggesting that their customers donate food to their employees at holiday time. Some women who work for Walmart have to sleep in their cars in the parking lot. And now, Walmart is the largest company in America with sales of almost a half a TRILLION dollars a year. Meanwhile the Waltons buy expensive homes and art, etc. In my opinion, the Waltons have redefined what it means to be "filthy rich." That term used to simply mean anyone with a lot of money. I have no objection to anyone making a lot of money. But when billionaires like the Waltons make their money by paying their employees less than they can live on, forcing them to apply for food stamps as a result, that is, in my mind the behavior of the "FILTHY" rich. The widow of Sam Walton is now the wealthiest woman in America and is building a multimillion dollar art museum near her home in rural Arkansas, buying million dollar paintings. As Jeff Goldberg (The Atlantic Magazine) said, "Ms. Walton's response so far to the needs of the people whose sweat pays for her paintings is a simple one, "Let them eat art." Walmart knows that their employees cannot make a decent living on their salaries and as a result, are forced to use government assistance. But that does not seem to concern the owners. So you and I end up helping Walmart pay their employees. Their actions are the epitome of pure GREED.

SOCIALISM, CAPITALISM and LEMONADE

Of course we already have, to some degree, a mixture of capitalism and socialism with programs such as Social Security, Medicare, farm subsidies, Unemployment Insurance, food stamps, the G.I. Bill, student loans for college and bank bailouts. Ironically, this relatively small amount of socialism is possibly what is preventing a revolution over too much 'free market" capitalism and a movement towards socialism. That is to say that without these safety net programs, people might be driven to go to the extreme and demand more government involvement during a serious recession, just as we have witnessed in Cuba and Russia. Franklin Roosevelt said that his greatest achievement was saving capitalism by instituting his socialistic programs. Because people tend to think that it has to be either socialism OR capitalism, they get scared even if there is a small movement in either direction. The Occupy Movement stands for a little more socialism, but not the kind that bailed out Wall Street.

When the Republican Governors Association met in November, 2011, one of their chief strategists, Frank Luntz, said flatly he was " So scared of this anti-Wall Street group; I'm scared to death. They (The Occupy Movement) are affecting what people think of capitalism." So he suggested replacing the word capitalism and calling it "economic freedom" or "free market." But the greed of the wolves on Wall Street, by any other name, is still greed. And even those not connected to the Occupy Movement are questioning capitalism. Many middle class folks are beginning to question where capitalism has taken us. And why not? We question and debate the education and the health care systems and even the American family system. Even many CEOs are growing nervous. They see the excesses of capitalism as unethical. They see that people trust business less and less. States require a "license to operate" a business but they also need a license from the people. And the people are not going to continue to let them operate when the overall wealth of the U.S. is increasing at the same time poverty levels are rising. That isn't fair or just.

Bill Gates' net worth is about $50 billion and is equal to the total wealth of 23 countries. We continue to worship at the altar of capitalism to the point of blindness. No one ever questions the ever-increasing unregulated capitalism at the expense of greater numbers of people. And we go to war to protect it. We have proven over and over that we will support a malevolent dictator who runs a capitalistic economy over a benevolent democratically elected president who has a socialistic economy. The two main ideas dominating our foreign policy since WWII have been stopping socialism and acquiring natural resources like oil, and both have been fueled by our blind worship of capitalism. We do not hesitate to go to war to further these two causes.

Meanwhile, the world keeps changing and so all systems should be questioned and debated, even capitalism itself; otherwise we will overlook the changes that might improve them. In a way of thinking, everything that the government spends money on is socialism isn't it? All expenditures are meant to help SOCIETY some way or other, aren't they? Unfortunately it is assumed that the economic systems of capitalism and "democratic socialism" are necessarily mutually exclusive. Although it is true that these concepts are polar opposites in their purest form, consider that it is possible for them to be mixed together in just the right amounts as to maximize the "general welfare."

Excuse a trite example but lemons and sugar are polar opposites, and yet when they are mixed JUST RIGHT, they make delicious lemonade. And you can vary the balance of the two to suit your taste, making the drink more tart or sweet. Not only can capitalism and socialism be mixed but they MUST be mixed.

Similarly, we can have as much or as little socialism as we choose; the amount is not carved in stone. Congress, if they are awake, can always increase or decrease the mix of the two as economic conditions change.

RUGGED INDIVIDUALISM and GOVERNMENT

Please understand that I clearly believe in individual responsibility, first and foremost. As Thomas Sowell said "No society ever thrived because it had a large and growing class of parasites living off those who produce." Rugged individualism has made America great. But we often forget that our greatness is also a result of being a society of cooperating communities. That's how we built the transcontinental railroad, won World War II, built the interstate highway system, put a man on the moon, developed the worldwide web and so on. It is also true that no society ever thrived when the disparity between the rich and poor was too great.

All of us, from individuals and corporations to our foreign allies need a little bit of temporary economic help from time to time. And "temporary" is the key word to emphasize. Federalist Paper #62 said "A good government implies two things: First, fidelity to the objective of government, which is the HAPPINESS of the people; secondly, a knowledge of the means by which that objective can be best attained." Note that the objective mentioned is HAPPINESS, not GDP, not security, nor equality.

The means by which that objective can be best attained is the subject of this work.

1

SOCIALISM IS IN THE EYE OF THE BEHOLDER

The American "empire" is in serious decline. We have a chronic recession, structural unemployment, growing poverty and a gigantic foreign debt and trade deficit. The Department of Education says that there are about one million school children who are homeless. How can we possibly be proud of our country?

Computerization and robots are displacing middle class jobs in the factory and in the office. Additionally, jobs continue to be shipped overseas. These trends will not change. This is partially why the employment rate is not improving at the same speed we've seen after past recessions. This truly is a national emergency, the first symptom of which is the Occupy Movement, and requires no less than an all-out war on joblessness and its resultant poverty. We have big economic problems and big problems require big government. This is not just another recession; there is a "sea change" in our economy which requires a sea change in government policy. So what I am trying to do here is open up the space to discuss socialism in a new way.

The very first concept we need to discuss (the elephant in the room) is that to some extent everyone is greedy. Many tend to think that only capitalists are greedy. But of course, greed is universal. Workers always want a raise and labor unions try to get a better deal with their capitalist bosses. And many attempt to "game" the tax code to minimize their tax liability. Welfare moms will game the system and corporations will do the same. Reagan's image of the "welfare queen driving a Cadillac" was a political exaggeration but it convinced a lot of folks that welfare was out of control and that it needed more regulation. And to some degree, they were right. Only problem was that they placed all the blame on the Democrats who originated these programs. However, the administration of those programs fell under the executive branch of government and were managed by both Republican and Democratic presidents during the sixties and seventies when program excesses began to be noticed and regulation needed to be tightened.

Those presidents did not regulate those programs sufficiently, resulting in fiscal sloppiness. The country as a whole was doing very well economically during those two decades, and there was plenty of money to go around. It is human nature that when there is plenty of money, people simply don't pay so much attention to waste. Somehow we think it is wrong for a poor person to game the system, but it's somewhat acceptable for the rich and corporations to do the same; that's just "capitalism" isn't it? Case in point, hardly anyone from the Wall Street banking cabal that unethically caused the great recession has gone to jail.

While Reagan was focusing on welfare fraud, the military-industrial complex that his Republican predecessor wanted us to focus on was going full speed ahead replete with fraudulence and corruption.

There is really nothing wrong with the government providing financial aid to individuals or companies temporarily if there is a return on investment (ROI). Problems come when there is not sufficient regulation of the programs, or Congress cannot agree on the existence or amount of the ROI, or a program keeps running perpetually after the need for it has past. These are the factors that give" socialistic capitalism" a bad name. But it need not be that way.

Self-interest simply dominates ALL of human activities. So let's face that fact. And if that is true, then we need to stop lamenting human nature, like Karl Marx did, and accept it by harnessing it and regulating it.

It should be quite clear now from what the 20th century taught us, that UNREGULATED pure laissez-faire capitalism simply doesn't work very well. We have seen how little regulation of Wall Street in the 1920's caused the stock market to crash and resulted in the Great Depression. More recently the same scenario played out with the lack of REGULATION of the mortgage lending business, causing the great recession of 2007-2013, with some fallout still continuing. Not surprisingly the resulting *income inequality* has been about the same in the "Great Recession" as it was during the Great Depression. It's not difficult to agree with French economist, former MIT professor Thomas Piketty's view that "Rising inequality is a built-in feature of capitalism, not an aberration." As Robert Reich suggests, "Although it is possible to win the lottery, the biggest lottery of all is what family you were born into. Our life chances are now determined to an unprecedented degree by the wealth and power of our parents." He goes on to say, "Taxes have been cut on the rich, public schools have deteriorated, higher education has become unaffordable for many, safety nets have been shredded, and the minimum wage has been allowed to drop 30 percent below where it was in 1968, adjusted for inflation. We have 20 million American children in poverty with the highest rate of child poverty of all developed nations."

Former Federal Reserve Bank Chairman Bernanke said that the great recession of 2008 is worse than the Great Depression. The underlying issue here is a moral one: What do we owe one another as members of the same society?"

F.D. ROOSEVELT AND SOCIALISM

It is clear from the last century that pure socialism hasn't worked well either, witness the Soviet Union and Cuba. The great recession of 2007-2012 would have been another depression if it were not for the socialistic safety nets instituted by F.D. Roosevelt's "New Deal" and L.B. Johnson's "Great Society" programs. Social Security, Unemployment Insurance, Medicare and food stamps, all contributed to saving the day in 2007-2012. We did not see people standing in soup lines or sleeping on sidewalks as we did in the early 1930's. The reason? Social Capitalism was at work! Had these social safety net programs already existed in 1930, the Great Depression would have just been another great recession. And if another free market capitalist like Hoover had been elected President in 1932, I am sure that there would have been a revolution. It is simple psychology. When a tipping point is reached and enough of the poor don't have enough food to eat they will start a physical war against the very rich, who benefit most from unregulated capitalism. FDR saved us from that revolt with his SOCIALISTIC programs, most of which he got implemented during the first 100 days of his administration. To say that capitalism and socialism, as I am defining it, cannot coexist within a government is just as illogical as saying that an individual cannot have both feelings of self-interest and feelings of charity for others. Quite often those two feelings are in conflict within us, just as they are in government.

A NEW KIND OF RECESSION

In some ways, capitalists and government have polar opposite goals. It goes without saying that companies create jobs. But at the same time, they are also unintentionally increasing the unemployment rate. That is, they are constantly looking for ways to reduce the number of employees they have. And the government is always working to increase the number of the employed. I am not saying that capitalists don't care about the country. It is just that in the name of efficiency and profitability, their job is to reduce employment in their own companies as much as possible. It is interesting to note that in the past, recessions went through a fairly predictable pattern. After several years of recession, the GDP and the stock market would finally start to increase, along with employment. There haven't been any indications since the beginning of this recession in 2008 that the normal patterns have returned. Here's the difference: since the top tier of society are most favorably affected by the stock market, their economists declared the recession was over in 2010. It was only over for the rich. There are still tens of millions unemployed, and now 46.5 million people are at or below the government-defined poverty line. There are 18 million vacant homes because of the foreclosures. Try telling those folks that the recession is over. In other words, because of the great disparities between the rich and poor today, the very definition of a recession is changing, depending on which class you are in. The rich class, in which most economists belong, are looking at the country from their own point of view, or mostly through the lens of the stock market. The greedy are not recognizing the plight of the needy. Conservatives are against governmental redistributive programs unless they are redistributing upward toward the top, as in bailing out the banks.

WHERE IS THE "SWEET SPOT"?

All humans possess some combination of both greed and empathy. Karl Marx and Fidel Castro did not understand the beneficial creative power of REGULATED greed. Their utopian views blinded them to the problems of pure socialism. The communists finally woke up in the last half of the 20th century. G.W. Bush and Herbert Hoover did not understand the destructive power of UNREGULATED greed. They had the utopian view that the free market, once it was released from the "shackles of government," would regulate itself and an era of uninterrupted economic growth would follow. Corporations are not people and they are all, by nature, very greedy. It is clear now that pure unregulated capitalism causes the economy to be built on unsustainable debt and will collapse resulting in high unemployment. I always found it amusing when G.W. Bush used to say "Let industry regulate itself." Either he was a fool who thought that might work, or he knew that it was ridiculous and was simply trying to trick people. Since even the fox is greedy, didn't he think that the fox should be the last to design the hen house?

Unregulated Wall Street is just as bad as unregulated welfare for the poor. Laissez-faire capitalism should be as dead as communism. Laissez-faire capitalism works very well for the rich but not for the poor or middle class. Corporations are not inherently evil; they are greedily doing what they're supposed to do for the benefit of their owners. The task of government is to balance socialism and capitalism by finding that "sweet spot" between them, such that the maximum common good is achieved for the maximum number of folks. What we need is something in the middle of these two extremes. To paraphrase Governor Jerry Brown of California: When navigating in a canoe, if you just paddle on the LEFT side all the time you end up going in a circle and if you just paddle on the RIGHT side, you also end up going in a circle. Obviously a little left paddling mixed in with a little on the right will keep you going straight ahead hopefully to some destination of happiness.

What **we need is better regulated greed (capitalism) and better regulated socialism.**

SOCIALISM REALLY IS IN THE EYE OF THE BEHOLDER

Let me continue to expand on what I mean by socialism. Anytime the government takes money from us and spends it on our common good, this IS socialism, isn't it? We the people pool our money into the

U.S. Treasury and it is redistributed to SOCIETY (us) in ways that our elected representatives feel is best for society as a whole. But if government spends money on something that we all agree is absolutely necessary, we don't call it socialism. So if government comes up with a program to protect the health of all Americans, we call it socialized medicine. But if the government creates a program to protect all Americans from foreign invaders, we don't call it "socialized defense," we call it the Defense Dept. We can't imagine not having a Defense Department, but Costa Rica and some other countries have none. They feel it is an unnecessary expense with no significant ROI. I'm not suggesting we don't need a military, I just want us to think about how much we spend on it.

Giving money to big banks, tax breaks for big corporations and paying farmers not to plant crops is socialism too. But we tend to use the word socialism for those expenses that we don't think are so necessary. As M.L. King said "When the government gives money to the poor, we call it a 'handout.' But when the government gives money to the rich, we call it a 'subsidy.'"

A simple example of an expense that we all agree on is the traffic light system used to regulate intersections. Traffic REGULATIONS require you to stop and spend time, which you'd rather not do, waiting for a green light. Additionally, the traffic lights cost you, through taxes, money which you'd rather not pay. But isn't the cost of regulation and taxes for the traffic lights worth it, given what the cost of all collisions and deaths would be if we didn't regulate traffic?

If the government had done a better job of REGULATING the poverty welfare programs in the 1960'-70's, Ronald Reagan would not have been able to convert so many Southern Democrats into Republicans by his famous quote "Welfare queens are driving Cadillacs." And if the government had regulated the banks better, the great recession would not have occurred. So liberals call giving money and big tax breaks to the banks and corporations SOCIALISM. And conservatives look the other way and call welfare for poor mothers with children SOCIALISM. The meaning of the word socialism depends on one's point of view, so it really is "in the eye of the beholder." When you define socialism this way it's not so scary a word is it? John Steinbeck said "Socialism never took root in America because the poor see themselves not as an exploited proletariat, but as temporarily embarrassed millionaires." Unfortunately the belief that anyone can become a millionaire in America is slowly eroding because lately the system is more and more rigged to the advantage of the rich, bringing about the largest disparities between rich and poor since the 1920's. The American dream can now only be found in our sleep!

THE MILITARY-INDUSTRIAL COMPLEX REDEFINED

The reason the poor and middle class no longer have as big a chance to become wealthy is something that President Eisenhower warned us about in the 1950's. But the military-industrial complex he spoke of has gotten much worse. It is now the military-industrial-banking-mainstream media-political lobbying complex. For example, when the military wants more fancy equipment, defense contractors enjoy filling that need and encourage it because it gives them more work and profit. The big banks enjoy being able to finance the big contractors during the interim before the government pays up. So if a reporter, discovers that contractors are building an expensive airplane that is not needed, and wants the editor of a big mainstream paper to publish the story, the editor tells the reporter that the story isn't worth telling because he knows that the folks who sit on the paper's board of directors may also sit on the contractor's board. And because the big Defense contractors are giving huge amounts of money to fund campaigns and pet causes of members of Congress, those Congressmen and women feel obliged to authorize more money for the Defense Dept. to build those unnecessary weapons.

So a vicious cycle keeps repeating itself. And who pays for all this wasted money? You and I do. Meanwhile the rich and powerful keep trying to increase the taxes on the poor while decreasing their own. Money follows power and power follows money.

DOMESTIC TRANQUILITY AND THE GENERAL WELFARE

It is my firm belief that all governments should have some combination of capitalism and democratic socialism to bring about the greatest "domestic tranquility" and promote the greatest "general welfare" as cited in the Constitution. But how can we have domestic tranquility when the assets of the top 1% are equal to the combined wealth of the bottom 40%? This is the result of the recent unregulated capitalism during the first decade of the 21st century. Welfare of just the top 1% is not the "general welfare" of which the founding fathers spoke. And people marching in the streets, the "Occupy Movement," is not the "tranquility" the founding fathers spoke of either. The Declaration of Independence was the first public assertion of human equality as a legitimate rationale for political action. The Declaration, little by little, caused the formal barriers of inequality to be eaten away; first it was race, then gender, religion, ethnicity, sexual orientation and any other differences that humans have created to hold some people down and raise others up. The long arc of history is going slowly in the direction of more socialism. But the trick is not to "paddle too much on the left." Regulation and proper taxation are the keys to making socialist and capitalistic systems work together. I hope you will feel that way too after reading this work.

2

THE LONG ARC OF
HUMAN HISTORY

To understand economic theory, it is necessary to understand human development. Back when we were living in small tribes, moving around, hunting and gathering, when grandma got too old to walk, the tribe just left her on the trail with a little food and water. They knew that she would eventually die from either starvation or being eaten alive by a wild animal. It literally was a "dog-eat-dog" world. Millennia later, we started burying our dead, an indicator of two developments: First that we stopped leaving the old and sick behind and secondly that we took the time to bury the dead. These were the first indicators that empathy was emerging as part of our human nature. Millennia later, we find graves decorated with shells and flowers, indicators that ritual and ceremony were practiced and a rudimentary celebration of the deceased's life suggested that empathy was continuing along its developmental path.

Eventually we learned how to sustain ourselves through agriculture and animal husbandry. This allowed us to have considerable resources, because we were not wasting time moving around. The extra time and resources allowed us to be more empathetic. Fast forward to today. Now we not only give our elders good food, housing and medical care, we also hold elaborate funerals to express our love, indicators of even higher levels of empathy. What has made our species so successful is the fact that we have learned to co-operate with each other so well. No claws or fangs were needed for five men WORKING TOGETHER socialistically with spears to take down the fiercest of wild animals.

A combination of empathy and socialistic cooperation has developed us into a successful species. Yet, it is tempting to say that the "survival of the fittest" Darwinian tendency is just as strong today as it was in the beginning by suggesting that the increased concern about others is just due to our greater amount of resources. That is, without all of our present day resources we would revert back to dog eat dog behavior.

STILL "DOG-EAT-DOG"?

However, there is plenty of evidence to the contrary. Examples that come to mind include survivors of the holocaust who relate that when many of the prisoners in their barracks were close to death from starvation, there were those who were able to share what little they had with those who were closer to death. They clearly were risking their lives to help the less fortunate.

Another true story, which as a former pilot really warms my heart, takes place during WWII when a lone German fighter pilot found a lone American bomber heading east over Europe. As he came in for the kill, he saw that the tail gunner and the top and belly gunners were dead, slumped over their machine guns. So as he approached closer, he could see that the cockpit was heavily damaged. The instrument panel, including the compass, was shot up too. Because it was a cloudy day and with no working compass, the American pilot could not tell that he was going east in the wrong direction and further into Germany instead of returning westward to England. The German could have easily finished off the bomber with one shot of his cannons. Knowing that the bomber could not shoot at him, the German, out of curiosity, pulled up beside the cockpit and was able to see the face of the American pilot. In that moment, his human empathy kicked in. Had he not seen the human face it was his job to kill, it would have been easier to shoot down another bomber plane. But he felt sorry for his fellow pilot, no longer thinking of him as the American enemy, BUT AS A FELLOW HUMAN BEING. So he started signaling with his hand that the American was going the wrong way. The surprised American knew he could easily be shot down and so had nothing to lose by following the

German's directions. The German pilot then accompanied him almost to the English Channel before turning back. By doing this the German went completely against his self-interest. By shooting down the bomber he would have added another kill to his record and helped his country win the war. By not doing so, he risked his life because heading towards England, he had no idea of how many other English or American fighter planes he might encounter. He also risked running out of fuel. And if Hitler knew what he had done, he would have personally tortured and killed his pilot with his bare hands. As if this story was not already incredible enough, after WWII the German pilot immigrated to Canada and settled in Vancouver. The American pilot was from Seattle and somehow they found out about each other, met and became the best of friends.

EMPATHY IS INNATE BUT ALSO LEARNED

We humans do have empathy for each other and it appears that over millennia empathy has slowly increased. Even so we continue to have difficulty understanding a disadvantaged person's point of view unless we have had firsthand experience of that disadvantage. For example, Jim Brady, one of President Reagan's closest advisers, was completely against any kind of gun control regulation. But after he was shot during an attempt on Reagan's life, he has since spent his entire life lobbying for more gun control laws.

Individuals of course vary tremendously in the amount of greed vs. empathy they possess, with Jesus, Gandhi, M.L. King, Mother Teresa and Nelson Mandela, just to mention a few, expressing great amounts of empathy, altruism, and charity.

We, on the other hand, remember the greedy capitalists only because of their fraudulent actions, excluding those like Warren Buffet and Bill Gates. If one could take all of the individual differences among people and average them to get a percentage of the amount of greed versus empathy expressed by the human race as a whole, my guess is that whatever the outcome of that ratio turned out to be, if altered slightly in the direction of more greed and less empathy, the whole human race would have self-destructed some time ago. (Of course it still could if some greedy dictator starts a nuclear war.) EMPATHY is the only glue that keeps us from killing each other more than we have. And empathy is the basis of Socialism.

Going back to our historical development, only 175 years ago, we Americans lived mostly in small farming and ranching communities. If a barn burned down, neighbors automatically went to help rebuild it. They were empathetic because they knew the importance of a barn to a family's livelihood. They also had a personal relationship with that family. This is socialism at work; it is unregulated socialism, but socialism nonetheless.

Consider this 21st century scenario: We learn that the great, great grandson of one of the original ranchers is now a very wealthy rancher. He has spent his whole life on one of the ranches located in Montana. Now instead of his neighbor's barn burning down, he reads that Detroit is burning down because the poor folks there are so frustrated with the unequal distribution of wealth and racial discrimination they are revolting. But he doesn't feel much empathy for them because those Americans are so different from him. They are mostly black city dwellers whose culture is so different. So when the government comes along and says, "Hey Mr. Rich Rancher, how about sharing some of your wealth to help these poor folks and use some of your money to set up job training programs in the inner city to "teach them how to fish" not give them a fish. And until they are trained and find jobs we want to use some of your money to feed them by providing food stamps and their poor grandmothers with medical care."

The German pilot story reminds us that it was easy to shoot down a plane when it was the target but not so easy to shoot when a human face came into view. So while the wealthy rancher might feel empathy for his white rancher neighbors, he may have difficulty feeling empathy for an anonymous little black kid growing up in Detroit living in a very poor and dysfunctional family. He may wonder, "Why can't these folks pull themselves up by their own bootstraps?" But it is hard to "pull yourself up by your bootstraps" when you cannot afford a pair of boots. Wouldn't it be better for all of society if that little boy had the benefit of a preschool education and socialization and after high school with some job training? Otherwise it is hard not to expect the boy will grow up discouraged and resort to drugs and crime. Plato said "The part can never be well unless the whole is well." And the reverse is also true that the whole cannot be well unless all the parts are well. Ironically, the rancher probably goes to church every Sunday and worships a Man who said, "As you did it unto one of the least of these, you did it unto me." Matthew 25:4.

3

ECONOMIC FORM IS NOT GOVERNMENTAL FORM

The two biggest mistakes that Karl Marx made were not understanding that human nature is basically greedy and that there was NOTHING he could do to change that. (I think Groucho Marx knew more about human nature than Karl Marx.) And, despite his hyper-socialist, read communist, economic system he did not anticipate that the future political leaders of Russia would end up as dictators just like the Czar who was assassinated by the oppressed masses. Unfortunately humans tend to go from one extreme to its opposite. Marx and his revolutionaries were so disgusted with the greedy dictatorship of the Czar (and I have seen his gilded palaces) that they thought that they could create a heaven on earth by setting up an economic system in which greed could not exist. Human nature doesn't change overnight; it takes millennia. Unfortunately they did not set up a government based on DEMOCRACY to manage their new socialistic ECONOMIC system. They created a single-party, authoritarian, autocratic governmental system with absolute power. Since "power corrupts, and absolute power corrupts absolutely," the well- intentioned new communist leaders gradually became dictators because there were no checks and balances that a democratic form of government would have brought them. Their greed naturally emerged.

Capitalism and socialism are ECONOMIC models not GOVERNMENTAL models. Unfortunately these two are often conflated, but they are separate. Consider that it is possible to have:
  a. A socialist economic system within a Democracy, like Denmark.
  b. A socialist economic system within a Dictatorship, like North Korea.
  c. A capitalistic economic system within a Dictatorship, like China
  d. A capitalistic economic system within a Democracy, like the U.S.

Most Americans conflate socialism with dictatorship based on what happened in Russia, and this is one of the main reasons that Americans are so afraid of socialism. And they conflate capitalism with democracy, as though they are inseparable and support each other.

WHAT IS THE ROLE OF GOVERNMENT?

We must have a better understanding and rapprochement in the U.S. between democratic socialism and capitalism WITH-IN our democratic system. By regulating both, we could identify a "sweet spot" to bring about harmony between the two and therefore create the maximum general welfare and domestic tranquility for the maximum number of citizens.

Sociologists recently questioned a cross-section of citizens in a number of countries, including the U.S., to determine levels of happiness. In 2010, the Paris-based Organization for Economic Co-operation and Development reported that Denmark turned out to be the happiest country in the world. Denmark is one of the most socialistic countries in Europe. Their taxes are high, nearly 50%. But college, medical care, city bus systems, and many other services are all free. 47.3% graduate from college, as compared to 36.5% in the U.S. There is very little income disparity and the Danes like it that way and are happier than we are in the U.S. The proof is in the pudding. Should not the "bottom line" measurement of a government's effectiveness be the level of happiness among its citizens, not just GDP?

If our present capitalistic system is not working very well, I am not recommending that we go as far as Denmark has in its level of socialistic approaches but I am saying that we need to stop fearing the concept of socialism.

Walter Russell said "Happiness is the indicator of BALANCE in the human machine." It is equally true that balance between greed and empathy can be an indicator of happiness. And it follows that a balance between capitalism and socialism would bring about more happiness. What good is it if we are the richest country and yet as a society as a whole, not very happy? The country of Bhutan has instituted a GNH instead of a GDP; a GNH or a Gross National Happiness index measures how well their government is doing to stimulate the conditions that foster happiness. They have their priorities straight. We must face the fact that we simply do not have the level of domestic tranquility and the sense of general welfare our forefathers envisioned when they established our country.

LAISSEZ-FAIRE CAPITALISM HAS NOT DELIVERED "THE GOODS"

In the last 80 years the U.S. has experienced at least 20 years of a very bad economy in the periods between 1929-1942 and 2007-2013 (And it's not over yet.) and that accounts for about 25% of the time, not including the numerous smaller recessions which occur with some regularity. One could say that capitalism only works about 75% of the time. Since human nature has not changed significantly during those 80 years, blame for those economic depressions and recessions must be laid not at the feet of the people but at the feet of the capitalist system and our government which tends to cherish unregulated capitalism.

If capitalism is the cause of the problem, then more socialism during the great recessions is the antidote. That is, if capitalism cannot consistently deliver STABLE general welfare and happiness, then the government MUST step in and deliver what the capitalists cannot seem to do. We Americans need to stop thinking that capitalism is the ONLY way, accepting that it naturally goes through cycles causing one painful recession after another. Would you accept wearing a shoe in which there was a thorn 25% of the time ? If you had a car or a refrigerator that only worked 75% of the time, would that be acceptable? We worship at the altar of capitalism so much that we just shrug our shoulders and accept that recessions are just a natural part of capitalism." I DO NOT BUY THAT ARGUMENT! If we can go to the moon, don't tell me that we cannot come up with a better economic system to either prevent recessions or at least greatly ameliorate them.

4

WHY GREED IS GOOD

I have been a management consultant for the last 39 years. And I have witnessed the benefits of greedy self-interest among my hundreds of clients. And I have experienced it myself. I will never forget the day I decided to start my company. I had been working for another management consulting firm, when at the age of thirty-seven I left and went out on my own. It was scary and exciting. I had a wife and two babies and very little savings. I was not making much money working for the other firm and I could see that the owners were getting rich. So the first couple of years, I probably worked 70 hours a week. But it started to pay off and I found myself earning twice as much as I had made as an employee. I eventually ended up with about 50 employees and earned 10 to 15 times what I had made before.

During these years as I would start to work with a new client, one of the first things I would ask him is "How

much net profit do you expect from your business?"
Usually they would say 5 to 15%. I only remember
one client out of a thousand who shocked me by saying 0%. He was a Mormon in Utah and he said that
he just wanted to create jobs for young men in that
town. The company was set up as profit-making business but in fact it was functioning as a charity.

I also noticed that my clients worked harder and
smarter when they owned the business than they did
working for someone else. For most employees, hard
work doesn't earn them as much as owning the business does. They are just not as motivated. When you
own your own business, it is nice to know that the
sky is the limit and that there is nothing to stop you
from making all of the money you can. Capitalism is
a great motivator and greedy self-interest is its powerful engine. However, since all business owners are
doing everything they can to increase profits by reducing their labor costs, they will buy technological
machines (robots and computers) to replace workers
and move manufacturing over-seas whenever they
can. It is also interesting to note that the reduction of
costs for labor in an individual company is a micro-
cosm of what is going on nationally in our oligarchic
power system. The oligarchs are using taxes and regulation to increase their share of the pie at the expense
of poor laborers.

Since all businesses are trying to reduce labor costs,
the owners are simply not interested in the overall

unemployment rate in the country. Although they don't consciously think about it, their priority is to *increase* the unemployment rate throughout the country. They think that overall unemployment is not their problem; it is government's problem. AND THEY ARE RIGHT. If not the government, then who?

5

WHO WANTS TO BE AN ENTREPRENEUR?

This is a subject that few talk about, but it is a very significant one. Let's focus on it. After my business became successful I just assumed that everyone would like to own their own business like me. However in the process of practicing my management consulting, I had the opportunity to personally interview thousands of employees in various companies. To my amazement, employees often stated that they didn't even want to be promoted into management. When I asked why, they said that they didn't want all of the "headaches" of managing people and budgets, etc., contrary to my belief that managing was "fun." The idea of starting their own business never entered their minds.

It slowly dawned on me that I was a somewhat rare breed because it appeared that only about 10%-15% of folks wanted to own their own businesses. That does not mean to say that more people don't dream about doing it, but when it comes down to it, they don't. This fact is SO important because if my theory is true, then what we are saying is that this ratio is simply a law of HUMAN NATURE. It never makes sense to set up political or economic systems that contradict human nature. Many capitalists seem to think that when there is high unemployment, the unemployed are to blame. They look at it from their own point of view and say, "Why don't they just get a job or start their own company like I did?"

But if it's true that at least 80% of people will never have the interest, guts, ability or the resources to start their own business, and if capitalism cannot, for whatever reason, seem to supply enough jobs for the 80%, then in the interest of the common good, what should be done?

If the capitalistic system cannot do the job of keeping people employed most of the time, then we the people, through our government, must step in and create jobs, at least temporarily, until the economy returns to full employment. And it does not matter what circumstances caused a severe recession; in the interest of morality and economics, we, the government, must step in and create jobs.

When the government does step in and create jobs, then people have money to buy goods and services from the capitalists. Henry Ford understood this and intentionally paid his workers high wages so that they could buy his cars. The problem comes when the government creates jobs which are not very useful. "Make work" programs are bad for the person doing them because he knows he is not really contributing much to society. And it is bad for the economy because the government is getting nothing in return for its investment. Unfortunately, "make work" programs are associated with the concept of socialism. But it doesn't have to be that way; the next chapter will provide some good examples.

PURE SOCIALISM DOESN'T WORK

I had the privilege of leading the very first delegation of small business owners from the U.S. to the Soviet Union in 1988. We met with Gorbachev's top economic advisers. I saw for myself what communism is like. Everybody was employed but everyone was lower middle class. I remember being surprised that on each floor of my hotel there was a woman at a little desk facing the elevator and her job was just to sit and watch. She had a job but it was not useful. It was a "make work" job. I went up to a taxicab driver and asked if he was busy. He was standing smoking a cigarette and his cab was empty. He said he could not take me because he was on a break. It was also against the law to tip anybody in the Soviet Union, including waiters and cab drivers. Just too capitalistic. So since the cab driver got paid the same amount no matter what and could not even take a tip, he had no motivation to drive the cab. I also noticed that on the busy crowded streets of Leningrad and Moscow nobody smiled or laughed. They all looked somber and hardly spoke to each other. I found the Soviet Union to be a depressing place. I felt like the people were generally depressed because living under their dictatorial government offered little in the way of economic capitalistic opportunity.

I saw why pure socialism simply won't work.

6

GOVERNMENT AS A JOB CREATOR

Whether or not you agree with the particular KIND of stimulus the government could use to create jobs, the more important question is HOW the government should go about it. You may remember Solyndra, a solar panel manufacturer, who declared bankruptcy in 2011. The government had loaned them $500 million as part of a program to bolster the solar industry. The government's assessment of how well this company would succeed was simply wrong. Having the government pick businesses to receive subsidies is not the best way. There are two reasons for this. First it is unfair to the competitors of the chosen business. And secondly, it disturbs the "invisible hand" of the market.

I believe that the invisible hand of the market works well, if regulated. So what the government should have done in the Solyndra case is give money directly to consumers, not the manufacturers or distributors. In this way, the integrity of the capitalistic system is kept intact. Consumers will decide which solar installers are the best and the solar installers will decide which distributors are best and they in turn will decide who are the best manufacturers. Letting consumers choose is a beautiful example of how capitalism and social- ism can be UNIFIED to bring about the greater com- mon good. The "invisible hand" of the capitalistic market is not interfered with and the socialistic func- tion is simplified.

Another benefit of this form of socialism is that it can be tied to the unemployment rate. For example, as the unemployment rate increased, the amount of money going to solar purchasers would increase and vice versa. When the rate went down to a level say of 4%, then all subsidies to solar buyers would fall to zero. The important point here is that many "socialistic wel- fare" programs need not go on forever. They should be used as medicine ONLY when the economy is sick.

Now you could say that although subsidizing renew- able energy this way does not disturb the internal functions of the solar business market, but doing so would be unfair to the petroleum industry. And you would be right. Yet sometimes in the evolution of cap- italism, one industry ends up dominating in an unfair way. When that happens, it makes it almost impos- sible for a newer player to enter the market. If we the people determine that has happened, then helping the

"Davids" against the "Goliaths" is in all of our best interests.

Right now, the oil and coal companies are so profitable that they are controlling Congress. In 2012 the oil companies had billions of dollars sitting in their accounts while getting tax breaks as they continued dumping their pollutants such as carbon dioxide into the air and petroleum by-products into our streams and soil and asking us taxpayers to pay for it. They continue to use their considerable amounts of money to influence Congress to kill any legislation that would help the renewable energy industry. In 85% of congressional races, he who has the most money wins.

There were in 2013 at least 28 registered lobbyists for every congressperson and an additional estimate of another 200 unregistered lobbyists. Clearly the fossil fuels industry needs to be more regulated and pay more taxes. Those extra taxes could be used to help consumers buy renewable energy systems. Every once in a while capitalism just doesn't work well, and if an industry gets too powerful, it's simply time to put it in its place.

7

USE OF TAXATION AND REGULATION

During my many years consulting with businesses, I was always amazed at how quickly owners would pivot from one practice to a new behavior simply because the tax code changed or a new regulation was put into effect. So although there are many ways to change people's economic behavior, I would think that taxing and regulating would be the principal ones. There are many examples that could fall under these two general catagories, but it would take a whole book to list them all.

I just want to mention a few so as to get some ideas percolating.

1) We need to greatly increase the income tax rate for people and companies who are the highest earners. The income tax rate under President Eisenhower was about 90% for the highest brackets. Eisenhower

certainly could not be called a socialist. Recently the Democrats had to fight tooth and nail just to get the highest rate raised from 35% to 39%. and Obama was labeled a socialist for that. If you ask the Socialist Party if Obama is a socialist, they will laugh at you.

THE ARGUMENT, COMMONLY PUT FORTH BY CONSERVATIVES, THAT DECREASING THE INCOME TAX RATE FOR SMALL BUSINESS WILL CREATE JOBS, IS FALSE.

I know that it seems counter intuitive to say that decreasing the income tax rate on small business will NOT create jobs. However the truth is that this is a myth the conservatives have institutionalized in America. I am incredulous when a Democrat remains silent in a debate with a Republican who espouses this theory. Either the Democrat believes this myth or simply doesn't know how to counter it. Part of the reason that the Republicans have gotten away with it, in my opinion, is that very few Democratic legislators have actually been small business owners, including Obama. More Republicans have owned small businesses than Democrats. Nobel prize winning economist Paul Krugman recently wrote that "Affluent taxpayers are likely to save the great bulk of ANY tax break" rather than spend it. So let us start with the premise that small business owners are in business to make all the money they can. Put yourself in the position of owning a small business during a recession.

Say you started out with about a hundred employees before the recession and now you've had to cut back to seventy. First of all, you probably are not making much of a profit (or none at all) because your business revenue is down 30%. But if you were making more than a profit of $250,000 a year and the government decided to reduce your income tax a small amount, what do you think you would do with that little bit of extra money? Would you use it to hire more employees and/or buy more equipment or land? Probably not. Why would you want to reduce your net profit by hiring employees you don't need. You just spent the last year "downsizing" and getting rid of employees. You will never hire more than the minimum number of employees needed to get the job done. Hiring more employees reduces your net profit. Additionally, why would you want to buy more equipment when about 30% of your equipment is now sitting idle. The truth is that you will only keep the minimum number of employees and equipment needed AT ANY GIVEN TIME to satisfy the amount of customers coming in the front door.

THE ONLY THING THAT WILL CAUSE YOU TO HIRE MORE PEOPLE IS IF THE NUMBER OF PEOPLE BUYING YOUR PRODUCT OR SERVICE INCREASES.

Since the lower and middle class simply have no disposable income in a recession, they are not going to increase their purchases of your product or service. So this creates a vicious cycle: consumers having little money to buy, means no increase in employment. No increase in jobs equals no money in the hands of consumers to buy anything. Conservatives argue THAT INCREASING INCOME TAXES ON BUSINESS IS A JOB KILLER. But this is just another form of the "trickle-down trickery." NEITHER A TAX BREAK NOR A TAX INCREASE on business will significantly AFFECT EMPLOYMENT. It simply will not increase the number of jobs because business owners will most likely put any extra money into savings. Remember that the income tax only applies to the surplus money left over after paying for all of the materials and labor costs. The surplus is the net profit. So if all of the costs of a company are already paid for, taking away, i.e., taxing, some of the net profit of the entrepreneur will have no effect on the business. The only thing that will create jobs is if the lower/middle class have money for purchases. When they do, the business owner will immediately start hiring more employees to satisfy the increase in demand for goods and services. This is trickle-up economics; trickle down never works as well as trickle-up.

2) The financial industry needs more regulation. Lack of regulation got us into the Depression of '29 and then again in 2007. Nobody disagrees with this except the folks on Wall Street.

3) A September 2013, Rasmussen poll showed that about 55% of Americans favor more regulation of the

coal industry even if it raises fuel costs. This is an indication that the people are thinking ahead of the government. We need to regulate the coal industry; it is the dirtiest source of energy in the world. Wouldn't it be "divine justice" to have a law that says that CEOs of coal companies must reside within a mile downwind of their largest coal plant so they can be sure to inhale the mercury those poor local residents have been breathing for years. A Texas study proved that children born downwind of coal fired power plants have lower IQs from breathing mercury emissions. And while we're at it, let's require that CEOs of nuclear power plants live close by as well.

4) Some capitalists believe all governmental regulations should be abolished. There are thousands of regulations for example governing the airlines. They relate to the safety of the aircraft and the safety of the pilots. Who among us would want to reduce the number of those regulations. And if so, which ones would you choose to eliminate before taking your next flight. How about the one that says that if a pilot is caught flying while intoxicated he loses his license for life. Regulations are absolutely necessary in a capitalistic economy because capitalists will ALWAYS put the cheapest and least amount of materials or labor into any product or service. Do you want to fly in a poorly built aircraft with marginally certified pilots?

5) As a portion of their income taxes, American families are paying about $6000 annually in subsidies to

U.S. corporations that have doubled profits and cut taxes in half in the last ten years while eliminating 2.9 million jobs and adding almost as many jobs overseas. The corporations need to start paying their fair share of TAXES. Polls show that the public agrees. I recently saw a bumper sticker that said, "Freedom is not free; Stop whining and pay your taxes." This is another example where the people are thinking way ahead of their government.

6) If we increased taxes on fossil fuel companies and regulated the emissions of carbon into the atmosphere, make them pay for dumping their gaseous garbage in our backyard and then took that same amount of money and used it to subsidize renewable energy in the manner I will discuss in the next chapter, then everyone would have jobs, we'd clean up the environment, and we'd reduce the need for war to control oil and gas in the Middle East. Incidentally, a large foreign-owned oil company that had the largest oil spill ever to foul the Gulf of Mexico is running an ad that says, "Creating jobs is a key part of our commitment to America." How stupid do they think we are? NO CORPORATION EVER TRIES TO CREATE JOBS. They are constantly trying to eliminate them.

7) In 1990 I was a candidate for the state legislature in California. There was a debate going on as to whether or not to force motorcycle riders to wear helmets. I was having trouble deciding which way to go on that issue because one part of me thought, why regulate

something that just affects the individuals? If people want to risk getting hurt, that should be their business, since it doesn't appear to hurt anyone else. Then, while on a tour bus in Spain, I witnessed a young woman on a motorbike run headlong into a car and be thrown over the car and land on her head, with out a helmet. My natural empathy kicked in and I realized that regulating what others might do to harm themselves could benefit society in the long run, given the costs for care and insurance that society ends up paying because the cyclist probably has no medical insurance.

The CA helmet law passed and has saved many lives and protected against permanent disabilities. This is an example of where socialism not only helps individuals but also society as a whole.

8) The minimum wage has not gone up in inflation-adjusted dollars. It was $2 an hour in 1964 which equals about $12 an hour in 2013. So the minimum wage has actually decreased while wages of CEO'S have increased in some cases to 350 times the amount their workers make per hour. We need to increase the minimum wage to at least $12 per hour.

9) What if we democratize the big corporations? Since States create and license corporations, it should be perfectly legal for the state legislators to pass a law saying that, for example, at least a third of all board of directors must be employees chosen by their peers in those larger corporations. Why is this important?

Big corporations are more powerful than Congress because they are controlling Congress. Even though a one-third employee minority could not control the corporations, it could influence them because employees know and understand the business in some ways better than the CEO and the top managers do. In addition, if wealthy stockholders were split on a decision, an employee contingent could break the tie, probably in favor of society as a whole. In Germany they have something similar called a "Works Council." How about a law saying that in Corporations with 1000 or more employees, the CEO can not earn more than 100 times as much as the lowest paid employee. Makes me wonder if the CEO's would want to raise the lowest paid rates to enable them to increase their own pay.

10) Also, why not have the government loan money to individuals who want to start their own cooperative company. That is, a company completely owned by the employees with each employee owning one share of stock.

If you think my proposing more socialistic policies on our capitalist system is radical, well they are not nearly as radical as the socialization that Abe Lincoln instituted in our economy. The plantation owners of the South were living in the lap of luxury because they had the most ideal free market, capitalistic system one could imagine. When your labor is free, how can you help but make millions? They were oligarchs and when it looked like the federal government was going to make them start paying their laborers, they fought back. They did not use lobbyists as they do today, they used guns; 618,000 men died in that dispute over what form of capitalism we should have. The Emancipation Proclamation was the height of socialism. And as a matter of fact, Karl Marx was cheering Lincoln on as he and Congress raised the minimum wage from zero to the going wage for farm workers. Why did the government interfere with the completely free market capitalism in the plantation industry?

Because it was IMMORAL!

Today we have a similar situation. Walmart, for example, (and this applies to all similar companies) is run like a slave owning business. What do I mean?

The period from 2007 to 2013, was a gigantic boon for Walmart because the country was going through the Great Recession. The two main reasons for the boon were that:

1) Middle class people who before went to more "high class" stores were pinched economically and started buying at Walmart. If one can increase sales, profits increase.

2)The second reason is that in a recession, there are not enough jobs to go around and that allows employers like Walmart to pay employees less, because they and their employees both know that a job that pays poorly is better than no job at all. So their employees stay with them at low pay because they feel they are trapped by the economic situation; and they are.

So Walmart got more sales revenue and cut their labor costs at the same time. That's a capitalist's dream situation. But it is the "perfect storm" for employees. It results in a form of de-facto slavery.

So what to do, if anything, about that? Mr. Walton could argue that neither of these two phenomena were caused by him. They were caused by the overall economy going bad. And he would be right. But does that make it morally right for Walmart to take such a huge advantage of the situation even though it is legal? Slavery was legal too.

Meanwhile, Mrs. Walton who is the richest woman in America is spending tens of millions on art for a museum near her house in Arkansas. I wonder if she knows or cares that some of her female employees are so poor that they are sleeping in their cars in the Walmart parking lots and that some of her stores were asking her customers to donate food to her poor employees?

Maybe it IS time for some new radical ideas because our country is sick, both economically and politically. We are in a long term decline. And with the gridlock in Congress I don't see much change in near future. So there have been and always will be times when radical measures to change the status quo are absolutely necessary. Weren't the men who illegally boarded the British ships and threw tea into the Boston Harbor, radicals? They were protesting "Taxation without Representation" and they needed to get the attention of the monarchy across "The Pond." And we know their radical behavior sowed the seeds for democracy. It is ironic that 21st Century poor and middle class citizens now feel like they are being taxed without representation because the rich have so much control over Congress. It is also ironic that present day "Tea Party" members would not call themselves radicals since they named their organization after radicals.

If you have a tree that is sick and you have trimmed it, watered it and treated it with the right fertilizer and medicine and it still is dying, there is no recourse except to pull it up by its roots. That is radicalism; the English word root comes from the Latin, radix. Laissez-faire capitalism is a sick tree. It needs to be pulled up by its roots and replaced with Democratic Social Capitalism.

10) You don't even need Economics 101 to understand that if capitalism is working as hard as it can, and it always is, and still cannot provide enough jobs, then it is obvious that the moral thing to do is for the government to step in to create those jobs. Isn't that better than paying millions of people unemployment insurance while they sit on their hands and become more and more discouraged? When there are plenty of jobs on Main Street, the economy takes care of itself.

In 2013 however, the conservatives in Congress are focusing on the wrong problem. They are focusing on the national debt which has grown tremendously during the last ten years. What they don't seem to realize is that 3 trillion dollars was spent on unnecessary wars in the Middle East and the mortgage bubble on Wall Street. Both of these problems were caused by policies of G. W. Bush, leader of those same conservatives.

We cannot ever get back the money we've wasted on the Middle East. Present-day conservatives want to cut the social welfare programs just when they are needed most. They still believe what Reagan told them about welfare mothers driving Cadillacs when they should be focusing on creating jobs. Furthermore, even if they are ignorant of the fact that renewable energy is the best infrastructure program to stimulate the economy and get everyone back to work, surely they must realize there other more traditional infrastructure problems that could be solved. We have more potholes than all the roads in Europe. We have bridges that are on the brink of collapse, school buildings needing major repairs, not to speak of the rebuilding needed after so many natural disasters.

11) Make all state colleges free. That's right, free. Highly educated folks are immigrating to the U.S. in unprecedented numbers. Wouldn't it be more cost-effective to put tax money into American education rather than to subsidize welfare programs? Besides,

the Federal government already has four free universities, namely the four military academies. If the Federal government can do that, why not the states?

Computers and Robots are taking over jobs and that trend is accelerating rapidly. We won't need so many blue collar workers since robots and computers are replacing them. Robots are now even building robots. No use lamenting this trend. Capitalists will continue to increase the use of robots because they are much cheaper than blue collar humans. So we'll need more college educated workers.

According to economist Enrico Moretti, University of California, Berkeley, the 2012 GDP in the manufacturing sector is double that of 1980, yet the number of manufacturing workers in 2012 is half the number than in 1980. He also says that each hi-tech worker creates about five jobs in the local service sector; restaurant workers are a good example.

What we will need is more engineers who can invent and design robots and computers. Free college would provide us with many more engineers and computer specialists, as well as improving the general education level of the country. In one of my wife's leadership training programs she uses the following quote to generate discussion: "The factory of the future will have only two employees, a man and a dog. The man will be there to feed the dog. The dog will be there to make sure that the man doesn't touch the equipment."

12) A Wells Fargo survey said that 34% of older people expect to work until they drop because of the bad economy. They simply can't retire like most folks could thirty years ago. Over the last thirty years, working families have been beaten up pretty badly. If we want a real middle class, then we must take the retirement crisis seriously. Seniors have worked their entire lives and have paid into the system, but now, more people than ever are on the brink of financial disaster and cannot retire. That is why we need to increase Social Security by at least 5%, not cut it as the conservatives want to do. Also, we need to increase the Social Security tax to include those with incomes up to $500,000.

A recent Rasmussen survey found that 53% of Americans say that America's best times are behind us. And another 17% are not sure. That totals 70% having no confidence in our capitalistic government.

13) We need to make sure that poor people have housing. It is a disgrace that in this country there are billionaires and homeless children living side by side. If Jimmy Carter can take volunteers and build houses, why can't we take the homeless and have them build their own houses? Can we Americans really call ourselves CIVILIZED to allow such an incredible disparity? When the unemployment rate is over 5%, the government must stimulate the economy by creating jobs, jobs, jobs!

14) We need to cut our wasteful spending on defense. America accounts for 50% of the world's defense

spending yet we make up only 5% of the world's population. Why do we need military bases all over the world? What are they doing there? Who elected us as the world's police force? Our expansion of troops around the world is reminiscent of the Roman empire before it collapsed. Will we ever learn from history? Where is the return on investment?

As M.L. King said "We have guided missiles and misguided men." Every dollar we spend on stationing soldiers overseas robs us of a dollar here at home.

15) We need universal preschool child care education paid for by the government. I started the first ever 24hr/7day a week child care center for factory women working the night shift. The women were so much happier to know their children were well taken care of on the midnight shift that they started producing more product per hour. Their absentee rate also went down. It was a win-win for the company and the employees.

16) Last but not least, we need to greatly increase the capital gains taxes. Even Warren Buffet agrees. But the conclusive evidence for that comes from the famous economist Thomas Piketty. He studied two-hundred years of capitalism in Europe and the United States and he came to the conclusion that our tax and regulatory laws benefit the wealthy much more than wage earning employees. And here is the critical part. The benefits are CUMULATIVE. This causes the rich to get richer exponentially. It works just like compounded interest.

But the compounding of interest is not just in dollars. As a person amasses more and more capital, he gets invited to be part of the power structure in Congress. Because of that, he is able to know things that the average person would not and is therefore able to make even better investments. And the more money he makes, the more politicians do his bidding.

A perfect example of that today is the Koch brothers. Their inherited wealth funds Republican candidates as well as those who are "buying" their longevity in Congress.

Free market capitalism says "Let the chips fall where they may." Well we all know now where those chips will fall; they fall into the pockets of the already rich. Piketty says the only way to stop this unequal process, which is feeding on itself, is to impose a progressive capital gains tax and even tax the capital itself. I completely agree. With that money we could start lowering the national debt and using some of it to invest in job creation such as a massive renewable energy program.

These are just a few "socialistic" ideas to open the discussion. But isn't it better to debate capitalism without settling it than it is to settle on capitalism without debating it?

The next idea is, by far, the best. And if you ask me how government could pay for all of this, my answer would be simple, by asking the question, "How did we pay for WWII after twelve years of a depression???"

8

JOBS, JOBS, JOBS

As I have said, the most important socialistic thing that the government can do during a recession, is create jobs. But the government doesn't need to create government jobs like FDR did. What our government must do is look at the economy from a long range point of view and see what is needed on the horizon. Most capitalists are near-sighted and are only concerned about the near future, quarterly profits, etc. George W. Bush amazed me when he advocated a tax rebate for people buying Hummers. He said it would stimulate the economy. These vehicles drink gas like a drunken sailor drinks rum. Using more foreign oil is not the type of government incentive we should give. So let me suggest a perfect economic rejuvenation program; a good example of SOCIAL CAPITALISM.

Such a program should benefit not only the workers, but also create NEW capitalists. It should not only benefit the economy, but also the environment and foreign policy as well. There is only one such program that would do all of that simultaneously in the second decade of the 21st century. So let us look down the road a bit and see what we need. We need: JOBS (When everyone has a good job the capitalistic economy works well, and less socialism is needed.)

CLEAN ENVIRONMENT (What good is it if everyone has a job but is getting sick and dying at a younger age because of the pollution of our environment.) It has just been discovered that the fish in the Pacific are now radioactive because the Japanese "played with the devils fire" at Fukushima instead of using the "sun god's fire" (Solar). And who knows what the lives of our children will be like if the climate keeps changing? Fossil fuels are the main cause of pollution and climate change, so we need to

DEVELOP ALTERNATE FORMS OF RENEWABLE ENERGY.

GET OUT OF INTERMINABLE WARS in the Middle East. It is now crystal clear that the main reason that we invaded Iraq and have remained in Afghanistan was and is to control oil and gas in the entire Middle East. Notice I did not say to get oil out of Iraq.

GET IDLE RUSTBELT FACTORIES HUMMING AGAIN.

So what kind of government program could solve all of these problems simultaneously? What it will take is a massive government economic rejuvenation program; but time and again some people in Congress stand in the way. They say that the deficit is too high. Nevertheless, how did we go to war and beat Japan and Germany in less than four years with a high deficit, no money in the Treasury and little or no military? What we need is a **big, bold, easy-to-understand** plan that about 75% of voters can agree on. Obama's previous economic stimuli were too scattered. If you ask someone on Main Street to explain Obama's stimulus ideas, s/he would be hard pressed to remember them, but would be quick to say that they were not enough to be significant anyway, and therefore possibly wasteful.

So what *would* be a big bold vision that about 75% of all Americans could agree upon?

About 75% agree we need a lot more jobs; about 75% agree that burning fossil fuels is probably responsible for most of the pollution in the air and climate change; about 75% believe that we should be energy independent; about 75% say we need to re-industrialize the country and about 75% say that we need a lot more renewable energy. A September, 2012 Fortune magazine poll consisting of 40% Republicans, 40% Independents, and only 20% Democrats, indicated that 74% said that the government should be playing a bigger role in stimulating the economy.

IT'S A NO-BRAINER!

Put all those factors together and the answer is a **no-brainer.** There is only one big, bold idea that satisfies ALL these criteria for the first half of this century and that is a **massive renewable energy program**. It would reinvigorate the economy, literally putting everyone in America back to work almost overnight, just as World War II did.

We need to declare war on our dependence on Middle East oil. Such a war would create manufacturing jobs, and new manufacturing companies just like WWII did. It would make us independent of Arab oil and the wars that Arab oil causes, and it would simultaneously clean up the environment. We're running out of cheap oil: sooner or later we'll be forced to produce exponentially more renewable energy, so why not start now? We should have started immediately after the Arab oil embargoes of the 1970s. We didn't, and now we need to realize the immediacy of our need **and act on it.**

That's why I call this a **massive** renewable energy **plan**. It would need the breadth and scope similar to the Manhattan Project that quickly developed the atomic bomb, or the jobs programs of FDR, or Kennedy's pledge to get a man on the moon ahead of the Russians within a decade. All these plans were considered completely impossible at the time they were announced.

The usual objection to renewables is that extensive research must be done **before** renewable energy is economically viable, is false. The truth is that renewable energy is economically viable and functional now. I have owned three homes outfitted with solar energy and they work just fine. There is just a lack of political will. Obviously research should continue. But we can't put off the inevitable and wait while we work out the "bugs." Millions can go to work to research, create, and implement solutions *today*.

If all of the hidden costs of oil and coal are added onto a gallon of gas, including cleaning up the environment, treating health issues related to the use of carbon-based fuels, waging wars to guarantee "our continuous supply of oil," and the cost of patrolling the Straits of Hormuz to keep the oil shipping lanes open, you'd find that fossil fuels are just as expensive as renewables, if not more. Of course the oil and coal companies don't want us to know about these hidden costs that we tax payers are paying.

Other countries already outstrip us in their use of renewable technologies:
* Israel has more solar energy per capita than the United States.
* Scotland converts more wave energy from the ocean than the United States.
* China and Denmark create and utilize more wind energy per capita than the U.S.

* China manufactures more solar panels than the United States—and they ship huge numbers of them for installation in the United States.
* Brazil converts more bio-energy (from plants) than the United States.
* Germany just outlawed nuclear power plants.

So while we are slavishly, and at great expense in cash and blood, protecting oil in the Middle East for the countries mentioned above, as well as ourselves, we fall behind in the renewable energy race.

Another argument against renewables is the upfront cost to transition from fossil fuels to renewable energy. And with the national debt we have today it would be difficult to persuade anyone to now spend our already diminished capital. **But jobs are always more important than debt. Every armament manufacturer, every steel mill and every warship builder knew this when World War II started.** Abraham Lincoln said "Labor is more important than capital." For every manufacturing job created, two other support jobs are created. If everyone has a job, then capital takes care of itself. If all the capital is concentrated on Wall Street while the folks on Main Street are jobless, how does that make economic sense? True societal wealth comes from people on Main Street working and producing useful goods and services, not from people on Wall Street "playing with money," just moving it around.

When Japan bombed Pearl Harbor, we had no money in the Treasury and the national debt was high because of the Great Depression, but we were still able to transition from a peacetime economy to a wartime economy overnight. We had no Army or Navy to speak of when the war started. Yet it took less than four years to win against Japan and Germany. In 1941 the United States had one of the weakest military forces in the world. Yet in three years and nine months we were by far the strongest country in the world, not only militarily, but economically. We didn't worry about where we got the money to fight the war; it just had to be done and we did it. By the way, Dick Cheney has been quoted as saying "Deficits don't matter." To him, deficits didn't matter as long as we were going to use more money to fight **for** Middle Eastern oil, but they do seem to matter if we need the money to fight a war against our **dependence** on that oil. And speaking of ridiculous ironic contradictions, in 2014, Rex Tillerson, CEO of Exxon-Mobil is suing the transcontinental tar sands pipeline because it runs too close to his house. Yet his company is a major supporter of the pipeline. Mr. Tillerson doesn't seem to be concerned about the hundreds (if not thousands) of other people who will have to live with this pipeline; just himself. Another example of the height of greed.

Many conservatives ridiculed Franklin Roosevelt's New Deal "stimulus plans" saying they didn't do much and that what really pulled us out of the Depression was the war. They don't seem to realize that the war itself was nothing more than a big bold economic stimulus package. Many felt it was forced on us, but it still was an economic stimulus package. Must it take a shooting war to get us going in a different direction? Economist Paul Krugman said "No country has driven itself into a debt crisis with a stimulus—nor has any country with significant debt regained investor confidence through austerity." Can you imagine what would have happened to all of the conservatives in Congress had they said to President Roosevelt, "Sorry, we are not willing to declare war on Germany, Japan, and Italy **because** we don't have the money right now and we don't want to run up the deficit."

I imagine the same thing would happen to conservatives in Congress now **when** the American people wake up to the fact that we need to declare war on our oil dependence. And by the way, taking an idea from World War II, couldn't we help finance such a project by recreating a war bond style program; call it an "Energy War Bond."

Stop and think about it; we got nothing from the money spent and lives lost in WWII. All the metal we mined and turned into weapons ended up overseas. All the money we spent on soldiers' pay was not recovered. We did not get any houses or refrigerators or cars or anything "useful." We ended up with nothing economically to show for declaring war on Germany and Japan. But the unintended consequence was full employment with many more people paying taxes rather than taxpayers paying for unemployment benefits. If we declared war on our foreign oil habit, and spent the same amount of money we did in World War II for four years, we'd have much to show for it:

1) An unemployment rate of LESS than 5% , like we had during WWII
2) A much cleaner environment
3) Greatly reduced dependence on Arab oil
4) No wars with Arabs FOR oil
5) Re-industrialization of our country, as happened during WWII
6) Creation of many, NEW, small renewable energy BUSINESSES.

If you're thinking, "Yes, renewables would be nice but they don't always work. What? The sun is **always** shining somewhere; the wind **always** blows somewhere. Even on shady, calm days there would be so many different types of renewable energy devices functioning in tandem in so many places that enough energy would always be available to the grid. And generating electricity from the ocean is right around the corner. Furthermore, the existing fossil-fueled generators could continue as back up to augment the power grid.

What can be done about transportation, since vehicles use the most fossil fuel and cause most of the polluting? It's true that today's batteries simply will not carry a vehicle very far and research is needed. But there's a solution that doesn't require waiting for a better battery. Service stations could be converted to battery charging stations and 100% electric cars could be designed to have a large tray of batteries positioned underneath the floorboard. Drive in and a forklift type device takes your tray of spent batteries out and inserts a new tray of charged batteries. This would take less time than filling your car with gas, and you wouldn't need to get out of the car. The battery charging stations could be charged with solar, wind, or wave energy. The only fossil fuel needed would be a little oil to lubricate electric motors occasionally. This way we would also be saving our oil for aviation (the one area in which renewable energy will never work).

We need a goal of 80% renewable energy within ten years by declaring war on foreign oil dependence. It's the patriotic thing to do. Why wait ten or twenty years or more when we can do it now and create so many jobs and new small businesses in the process?

We cannot create the future by clinging to the past. If we could start with limited resources and win World War II in less than four years, do not tell me that we couldn't design, create, manufacture, and install renewable energy equipment in the United States in the same amount of time. In WWII we had three countries as enemies. Today our three enemies are:

(1) Big oil and coal interests **dominating** Congress
(2) **Ignorance** about renewable energy's usefulness *now*, and
(3) A lack of **political will** to do anything.

Some of the polls I've read show that about 79% of Americans are for renewable energy **now.** They wonder why we don't do it now. Are we really willing to continue allowing oil companies to kill renewable energy legislation out of their own **greed**? The American people **are** stronger than the oil companies when they have a plan that puts them to work. We saw what happened when simple ideas were understood. The question of a woman's right to vote was simple. The question of civil rights was simple: Should we outlaw racial discrimination or not? Could we put human beings on the moon in a decade, piggybacking off of infant or non-existent technologies? These were **big, bold**, easy-to-understand questions. The problem is that energy is not a simple problem. The public needs a lot more education about renewables and the renewable energy industries have been poor at explaining it.

If you present a **big, bold, understandable** program to completely revitalize the economy the people will be out in the streets supporting it. I have had a dream for the last 40 years since the first Arab oil embargo. I see solar panels on almost every building and windmills wherever there is consistent wind and ocean generators along our coasts and little or no imported oil, and no need for dirty tar sands oil, or nuclear energy as well. And during those whole 40 years the oil and coal companies have been secretly doing everything they can to stop the government from helping renewables take off.

We must look forward and act today, or continue to bury our heads in the sand; the sands of the Middle East. Implementing a massive renewable energy program is probably the best example of how socialistic capitalism could be used for our common good in the first half of the 21st century. But we also need to set up a permanent mechanism to generate an infinitely elastic demand for useful work, such that at any given time the number of folks looking for work is about equal to the number of jobs available. This kind of socialistic capitalism is a real GAME CHANGER and is an excellent example of the UNIFICATION of capitalism and socialistic policies.

9

SOCIALISTIC REVOLUTION?

"If a free society cannot help the many who are poor,
it cannot save the few that are rich."
John F. Kennedy

Notice that I did not say "SOCIALIST" revolution. I am talking about a revolution WITHIN the capitalistic system toward a greater degree of socialism but still preserving the basis of capitalism. One of the problems that those who mindlessly worship capitalism don't stop and think about is that capitalism does have some rules imposed upon it. There is no such thing as pure laissez-faire capitalism. When they say "Just leave the market alone and everything will work out best in the end", they forget that the rules (taxes and regulations) are now tilted to help the rich. That is of course because the big corporations are controlling Congress.

The system is no longer fair. It naturally allows the rich to grow richer and the poor, poorer. This is truer now than in the 1920's. There is growing misery among the exploited middle class. Masses of people find themselves excluded and marginalized, including a lot of college graduates without jobs, without hope and without a possible means of escape. Class struggle defines most of human history. Unfortunately we keep repeating it.

EARLY SIGNS OF A REVOLUTION IN THE MAKING

As a result, the country is now like a tinder box waiting for a spark, as evidenced by Occupy Wall Street. The rich and most members of Congress seem to be out of touch, although they should have had a wake-up call when Romney lost the 2012 presidential election so badly. The American people know something is very wrong but they just don't know exactly what it is. Well it is very simple. We've gone to the extreme with laissez-faire capitalism. Socialism used to be a "dirty word" but now capitalism is considered more and more a dirty word.

In 2013 the conservatives in Congress were trying to cut down the social safety nets, by reducing Social Security, food stamps and unemployment benefits. The rich don't seem realize that those programs are the only thing keeping the poor from "picking up their pitchforks" and storming their gated communities. Their ideology has gotten in the way of their common sense.

Thomas Jefferson said something to the effect that we should have a revolution every once in a while. The last one was in the 1960's. But as I said earlier, I think we still have enough socialistic safety net programs already in place which will prevent people from being hungry enough to use violence to change the system radically from capitalism to pure socialism. And that is a good thing, because if things get bad enough to cause a violent revolution, chances are that the new system would be TOO socialistic. It is unfortunate that human nature tends to bounce from one extreme to the other.

One of the ways to know if a revolution is coming is when some of the top people in the power structure start to defect. In recent revolutions in the Middle East, military generals and ministers previously aligned with the dictator in power, started defecting to the revolutionaries and that was a sure sign that the dictator's days were numbered. In our case, we have a multifaceted oligarchic dictatorship composed of the "Military-Industrial-Banking-Mainstream Media-Big Corporations-Political Lobbyist Complex."

Warren Buffet, one of the principal benefactors of the oligarchy has defected. He shocked Wall Street and the capitalists in Congress by saying that income taxes should be RAISED for him and his wealthy compatriots. For some time the rich have been accusing the poor of class warfare every time Progressives in Congress advocate that the rich need to be taxed more. But since it is the cabal of rich, powerful people and institutions that have slowly tilted the economy, thru taxes and lack of regulation, towards favoring the rich, in reality it is the rich who have started the class warfare. So as Warren Buffet aptly stated, "There IS a class warfare all right, but it is my class, the rich class, that is making the war." Then his son, Peter Buffet, recently said in a New York Times Op-Ed piece that capitalism needs a lot more humanism (read empathy). He said we need SYSTEMIC change and that "It's time for a new operating system, not a 2.0 or a 3.0 but something built from the ground up. New code." He continued, "What we have is a crisis of imagination. Money should be spent trying out concepts that shatter current structures and systems." In Buffet's NYT's piece, he stopped just short of saying capitalism needs to go. But in a later interview with Laura Flanders of Grit-TV he did say that capitalism as we know it must be radically re-worked. He was careful to not use the "S" word, but a wink and a nod between Laura and Peter told it all.

To the chagrin of many American conservatives who are Catholic, the new Pope Francis is now hinting at an economic revolution. The Pontiff's criticism of the modern capitalist economy is succinct and powerful. The Pope said "We need to reject the absolute autonomy of markets and confront the structural causes of inequality." And that until we do this,"No solution will be found for the world's problems." He asks the oligarchs to realize that to "Not share one's wealth with the poor is to steal from them." He further advises that "Thou shalt not have an economy of exclusion and inequality because such an economy kills." He laments the deified (capitalistic) market and says that "Unregulated financial capitalism causes a selfish and individualistic mindset." He calls for a "NEW ECONOMIC MODEL." He even explicitly criticized the "trickle down" economic theory. And then he fired all of the Cardinals managing the Vatican Bank when he found corruption. (Our oligarchy just gave our corrupt banks more money.) Finally he states that "No law enforcement or surveillance systems can indefinitely guarantee tranquility until we reverse the exclusion and inequality within society."

The Pope is clearly hinting at the possibility of a violent revolution of some kind. Then shortly after his speech, wealthy American Catholics like billionaire Kenneth Langone attacked the Pope saying that if he did not stop "bad mouthing" capitalism he would stop donating money to the Catholic Church. See how the oligarchy works!

Bill Moyers said recently that the oligarchs "Fix the system so multimillionaire hedge fund managers and private equity tycoons pay less of a tax rate on their income than school teachers, police, fire fighters, secretaries and janitors. They give subsidies to rich corporate farms but cut food stamps for working people facing hunger. They remove oversight of the "Wall Street casinos" but bail out the bankers who torpedo the economy, fight the modest reforms of Dodd-Frank, prolong tax havens for multinationals, and stick it to consumers while rewarding corporations. And who pays? We pay. We pay at the grocery store. We pay at the gas pump. We pay the taxes they write off. Our low wage workers pay with sweat and deprivation because Washington-aloof, self-obsessed, bought off and doing very well, thank you, feels no pain." He then ends by saying that "If the details of our corrupt system were exposed for what they are, outraged citizens would descend on Washington D.C. and tear it apart with their bare hands." That is pretty strong language from this mild mannered Texan and minister's son. And that sounds like revolution to me.

There will be a lot of marches in the streets, like Occupy Wall Street and the Million Mask March in 2013. They will come in "fits and starts" but they will continue, hopefully not violently. Presently, fast food workers are marching in the streets to protest their average pay because they just cannot live even humbly.

Unfortunately, Congress never has done anything important until there were marches in the street. A woman's right to vote and to choose an abortion were both preceded by big marches. The 1964 civil rights bills and the end of the Vietnam War followed big marches.

There is the story about a woman telling FDR that she appreciated something he was trying to do and he replied, "Yes but you (the people) must MAKE me do it."

There have always been politicians who are afraid to do anything controversial out of fear of losing their jobs. But it seems that nowadays most members of Congress are afraid, and the few that are not, are marginalized by their congressional peers and by the mainstream press. Congress has become ossified and writing to Congress will do little good. They will not do anything significant unless hundreds or thousands of people descend on their office, demanding change.

There is a general feeling that we need to change not just our politics, but also our collective consciousness and our whole social and economic system. A recent Rasmussen survey found that 53% of Americans say that America's best times are behind us. And another 17% are not sure. That totals 70% having no confidence in our capitalistic and governmental systems. We have swerved from the angels of our better nature. We are headed for a cliff. We simply can do better than the kind of capitalism we have been practicing which enriches the few at the expense of the poor and middle class.

We need to use socialism intensely during a recession and then scale it back when the economy returns to normal. Not only is that the morally right thing to do, it is also the right economical thing to do. Socialism is the antidote to laissez-faire capitalism and capitalism is the antidote to too much Socialism. Another way of putting it is to say that capitalism is basically good but it isn't ALL good. And socialism is not ALL bad. Albert Einstein, among other notables we admire, was a socialist. Plato said "Necessity is the mother of invention" and it is becoming clearer that we need to invent something better than the capitalist or socialist models. The unification of these two (which I am advocating) almost needs a new lexicon, a new name. It will be a NEW ECONOMY for the 21st century.

We are reaching a tipping point and are at an historic moment. We have become the government of the few, by the few and for the few. Congress is of the wealthy, by the wealthy, and for the wealthy. We are now ruled by an oligarchy. As Chris Hedges said "Oligarchs do not believe in self-sacrifice for the common good. They never have. They never will. They are the cancer of democracy."

But as Bob Dylan, the troubadour of the 1960's revolution, said,

> "The times they are a changin
> Cause the waters around you have grown;
> and you'd better start swimming
> or you'll sink like a stone,
> for the times they are a changing!"

And we had better start changing by judiciously applying more socialism. That is the key to preventing recessions and depressions and thereby bringing about a "sustainable" form of capitalism and in so doing, keeping the peace domestically. As Chris Hedges put it, "We are the most *illusioned* people on the planet. The sooner we realize that we are locked in a deadly warfare with the oligarchy, the sooner we will realize that these elites must be overthrown." He says that "Our inability to grasp the pathology of our oligarchic rulers is one of our gravest faults." Then he ends by saying "Let's get this class warfare started."

And it doesn't take that many people to start a movement. As Margaret Mead said, "Never doubt that a small group of thoughtful, committed citizens can change the world. Indeed, it is the ONLY thing that ever has." The tinder is very dry and ready for a spark.

We have nothing to fear from socialism, unless we let it get out of hand. And we have nothing to fear from capitalism, unless we let it get out of hand. The greatest guarantee of freedom is TRUTH.

In the land of lies,
The TRUTH IS ALWAYS REVOLUTIONARY,
and soon it will be realized that our oligarchic
emperor has no clothes.

ACKNOWLEDGEMENTS

FIRST I WOULD LIKE TO THANK THE PEOPLE WHO MOST INFLUENCED MY THINKING WHICH RESULTED IN THIS BOOK.

THEY ARE RICHARD D. WOLFF, PhD ECONOMIST; CHRISTOPHER HEDGES, FORMER CORRESPONDENT, N.Y. TIMES; PROFESSOR NOAM CHOMSKY, AND FELLOW TEXAN'S BILL MOYERS AND JIM HIGHTOWER.

I ALSO WANT TO THANK THOSE WHO ENCOURAGED ME: MY WIFE, MR. RAY HILLMAN, MR. GEOFF DEWAN, MR. THOM TYSON, MS. JESSIE BENTON AND MR. DICK RUSSELL.

I ALSO APPRECIATED THE ASSISTANCE OF MS. LAURA STEWART OF OUTSKIRTS PRESS.

CPSIA information can be obtained at www.ICGtesting.com
Printed in the USA
BVOW07s0041070714

358214BV00001B/36/P